THREE
COLOR
PAINTING

THREE
COLOR
PAINTING

STAN KAMINSKI

GUILD OF MASTER
CRAFTSMAN PUBLICATIONS

First published 2009 by
Guild of Master Craftsman Publications Ltd
Castle Place, 166 High Street,
Lewes, East Sussex BN7 1XU

ISBN 978-1-86108-664-8

Associate Publisher: Jonathan Bailey
Production Manager: Jim Bulley
Managing Editor: Gerrie Purcell
Editor: Gill Parris
Managing Art Editor: Gilda Pacitti
Designer: Simon Goggin

Set in Interstate

Color origination by GMC Reprographics
Printed and bound in Thailand by Kyodo Nation Printing

CONTENTS

GALLERY OF PAINTINGS IN **WATERCOLOR-STYLE GOUACHE**

GALLERY OF PAINTINGS IN
OIL PAINT-STYLE GOUACHE

Page 86: Golden Retriever

INTRODUCTION

In this book I share some of the knowledge, hints, and tips I have discovered over the years while training to be an illustrator in a design studio, as a freelance advertising illustrator, and as an artist and tutor. The advice given is suitable for the complete novice, someone who would like to learn to paint, but the experienced artist may also find some of the ideas useful.

Designers' gouache has been used for all the painting demonstrations in this book. However, because the principles are universal, the techniques discussed and the methods of working would translate equally well to watercolor, oil, or acrylic techniques.

A variety of subjects are included and there is photographic reference material for each demonstration to illustrate the points made. However, I do not show you how to copy a photograph or the scene in front of you, but how to understand what is happening in the scene and the way in which areas relate to each other tonally. I demonstrate how the most complicated scenes can be simplified and, if tackled in an organized way, broken down into logical tonal progressions.

When I started teaching using a full palette, I found students struggling with the practice of mixing colors. After a lifetime of painting this came to me quite easily, so I reduced the palette to the minimum of three colors, to make life easier.

Facing page: My wife Christine in Tenerife, with sky, sea, and an array of flowers and flesh tones. This is one of my first paintings using just three colors – here they are oil paints.

Below: "Eilean Donan" in the same three colors but using watered-down gouache. In spite of the varied details in the landscape, I was still able to produce a decent "watercolor-style" painting.

Ultramarine blue, yellow ocher and alizarin crimson are the only colors used for the demonstrations in this book. If the gouache is thinned down you can produce a "watercolor" effect but, with the addition of white and the paint used more thickly, an oil-painting effect can be achieved.

By experimenting with the mixes I found that the three colors harmonized well and that I could produce decent paintings with a wide range of color mixes.

Use your own reference material and try out the techniques yourself. There is no right or wrong way and the suggestions in this book are the basic rules I follow when I plan a painting. The three colors are a foundation to build on, a structure that can and should be modified and ignored in some instances.

Painting is a journey, so enjoy the trip. You'll find it liberating: three colors, two brushes, a palette to mix on, a water jar, and paper, and you've got a studio in your pocket!

GETTING STARTED

Materials, Equipment, and Techniques

MATERIALS AND EQUIPMENT

You don't need to spend much on art materials. Below is a list of the few items you will need to achieve impressive results following the techniques described.

You will need:

- Designers' gouache colors in ultramarine blue, alizarin crimson, yellow ocher
- Palette (e.g. an enamel plate)
- Water jar
- Bottle of masking fluid
- Roll of smooth, strong bathroom tissue (for cleaning the palette and lifting washes)
- Soft pencils (2B to 6B) for making a tracedown sheet and general drawing
- 2 hard pencils (2H and 3H) for tracing down
- Putty eraser for lifting off heavy pencil tracedown marks

Plus, for watered-down gouache

- 2 soft-haired brushes (sable is best): 1 wide, flat, ½in (12mm), 1 small round, size 3
- Good-quality watercolor paper (I use Bockingford 300gsm NOT paper. "NOT" means the surface of the paper is NOT rough). This paper does not need to be stretched.

Plus, for thicker gouache

- Designers' gouache in white
- 2 bristle brushes (hog hair is best): 1 wide flat ⅜in (10mm), 1 small flat ¼in (6mm) or less
- Good-quality watercolor boards (I use Saunders Waterford watercolor board and mountboard, in various colors)

TIPS AND TECHNIQUES

CUSTOMIZING A BRUSH

If you take your new, round sable brush which has a nice sharp point and cut the end off square with scissors, when wet, the end of the brush will flatten out and have some of the characteristics of a flat brush, but on a smaller scale (see below left). The beauty of a flat brush is its versatility: when wet it will flatten out, giving both a wide brush mark used flat on, a very fine controllable line when used side on, or a fluid, varied line when using the corner of the brush – it's like having three brushes in one.

Below left: Turned side on, the round sable brush comes to a nice sharp and very controllable point, as do the other brushes.

Below right: The small, sable brush on the left is a round brush with the tip cut off. When wet you can flatten the tip of the brush and it looks just like a small version of the larger flat brush next to it. The hog-hair brushes on the right are standard flat brushes.

PREFERRED PALETTE

For a palette I use an enamel plate, arrange my three colors on the outer rim and use the center of the plate to mix the colors on (see right). The recess makes it easy to wipe the palette clean and, because it's made from enamel it is light and will not break, so is ideal for outside use.

WHY GOUACHE?

Commercial artists use gouache for its versatility: it is water-based and has no odor; you can get watercolor effects by watering it down and using it on watercolor paper or board. Oil effects can be achieved by using gouache straight from the tube on white or colored boards, and any wash or texture in between. It dries instantly, but the colors on the palette are revivable when wet.

BRUSHRULING

To get really straight lines, use a sturdy plastic ruler to steady the brush, allowing it to be run along the ruler's edge (see below).

Above: Lean the ruler at an angle, supporting it with the fingers and the palm of one hand then, using the thumb to hold the ruler tight, rest the brush against it and use the fingers holding the brush to control the distance of the brush from the surface of the paper.

MAKING A TRACEDOWN SHEET

All the painting demonstrations in this book
are worked from photographs and, if you are
a complete novice and find copying difficult,
the easiest and quickest way to transfer the
photographic image to your painting surface
is with a home-made tracedown sheet.

I learnt how to make these when I began
work in an art studio, and have found
the technique very useful ever since.
The steps on here show you how to prepare
a tracedown sheet, while the instructions
on pages 20-21 show you how to transfer
an image onto your painting surface using
your tracedown sheet.

1. The equipment you need to make a tracedown sheet.

You will need:
- Sheet of tracing paper of a good weight
  (I use 90gsm)
- Can of lighter fluid (available from
  newsagents)
- A handful of cotton wool
- One or more soft pencils, the softer the
  better (4B-6B)

2. Rub pencil all over the tracing sheet in a random manner, to cover it.

3. Dampen cotton wool with lighter fluid.

4. Smudge pencil marks with damp cotton wool.

5. The finished tracedown sheet. If areas look a little light, go over them using the same process when dry (which takes a couple of minutes). Once the tracedown sheet is dry, it can be used over and over again, and should last quite a few years.

A Word of Warning

Prepare the tracedown sheet in a well-ventilated room, as the smell of the lighter fluid can be quite heady.

TRANSFERRING THE IMAGE

Don't worry if you can't draw accurately, as you can easily transfer a photographic image onto your painting surface using a homemade tracedown sheet (*see* pages 18-19).

The beauty of this technique is that it is a simple way to get started on even quite complicated subjects and achieve a good result. The tracing method will give you a good outline, but photocopies can be limited in clarity so you will have to use judgment as well. To get the most out of this process, look at your reference photograph while you trace down. You can then understand the shapes that you are tracing off and become familiar with the subject matter through observation. The more you understand what is happening in the scene, the better your painting will be. Take your chosen reference photograph to a photocopy shop and get a black and white copy made of the chosen area for your painting. The size of the photocopy can be up to 11 x 17in (A3), with the image filling the sheet; tracing off a sheet of this size will fit neatly onto a half imperial sheet of watercolor paper, allowing a generous margin for positioning a mount on the finished work.

1. An 11 x 17in (A3) black and white photocopy made from the reference photograph.

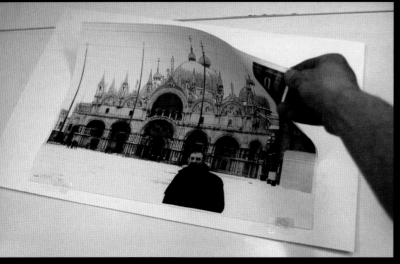

2. Use transparent adhesive tape to attach one side of the photocopy to your chosen painting surface. When removed, the tape could damage the surface, so attach it in an area that will be masked off, or where the damage will not be noticeable in the finished painting.

3. Place the tracedown sheet behind the photocopy, pencil-side facing the painting surface.

4. Using a hard pencil trace off the image on the photocopy onto the surface beneath. Continually refer to the reference photograph, so that you have a good understanding of the information the reference material contains. The better you understand what is happening in the reference, the more accomplished your painting will be.

5. Once the big shapes are in place, the detail can be filled in freehand, which will help build up your drawing skills. Put in as much detail as you feel comfortable with, and keep checking to make sure you are pressing down hard enough with your pencil for the image to transfer onto the paper.

MIXING COLOR WASHES

The three primary gouache colors used throughout this book – ultramarine blue, alizarin crimson and yellow ocher – can be thinned down with water to act like watercolor. The result may not be quite as smooth as watercolor (the pigment is coarser) but it is good enough to produce a watercolor effect.

When painting a wash over a large area, the paint needs to be wet enough to allow the paper to be covered without areas of color becoming dry. This allows a little time to add more color to the wash, or to carefully remove some color with bathroom tissue or clean water. Smaller areas should stay wet enough to allow manipulation – such as softening an edge – where appropriate. As a rule, the paint should be on the wet side rather than too dry, as drying time is thinking time.

The color wheel on the facing page shows the three "primary" colors: yellow at the top, blue to the left, and crimson to the right. The colors were placed on the paper and, while still wet, introduced to each other to create "secondary" colors: yellow and blue create a green, yellow and red an orange, red and blue a purple. The more yellow and water added to the green, the brighter the green becomes; the more blue mixed into the green the darker it becomes. The same principle works with the other mixes: the more red added to the purple the warmer it gets; the more blue the cooler it becomes; and the more water, the brighter the colors become. The secondary colors in the color wheel – green, orange, and purple – were then each run towards the center of the wheel and the "complementary" colors (i.e. those opposite them on the wheel) introduced. The green merged with the red creates light browns, the orange merged with the blue creates dark browns, and a little ocher added to the purple creates a strong dark color. By experimenting, thinning the mixes with water to make them brighter, and using the washes thicker to make them stronger, an amazing array of colors can be created.

These two swatches show the same three gouache colors that have been used throughout this book: yellow ocher, ultramarine blue, and alizarin crimson. Notice how the background color changes the appearance of the paint, so that the colors appear brighter on the dark blue board than they do on the white watercolor paper.

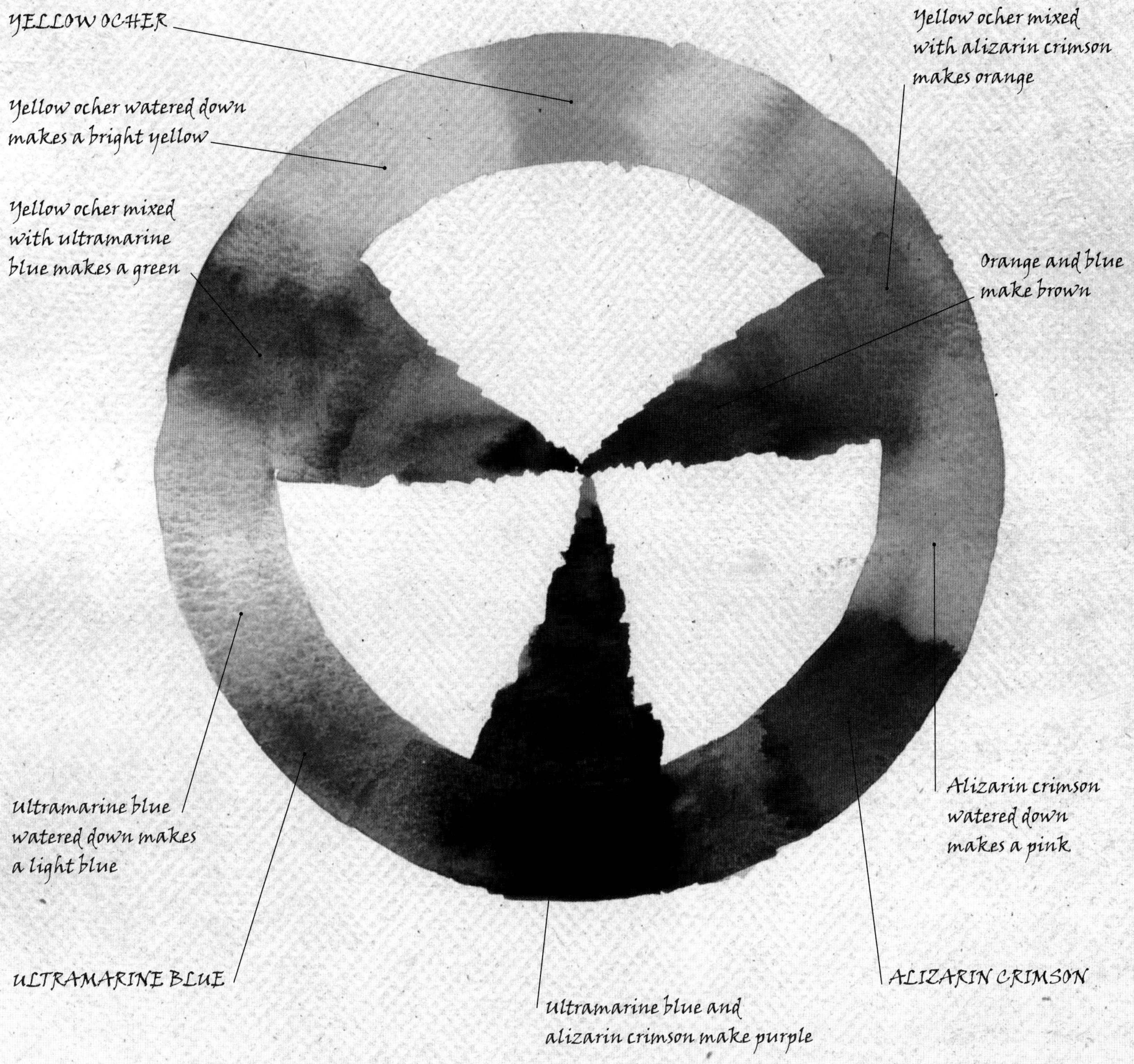

YELLOW OCHER

Yellow ocher watered down makes a bright yellow

Yellow ocher mixed with ultramarine blue makes a green

Ultramarine blue watered down makes a light blue

ULTRAMARINE BLUE

Yellow ocher mixed with alizarin crimson makes orange

Orange and blue make brown

Alizarin crimson watered down makes a pink

ALIZARIN CRIMSON

Ultramarine blue and alizarin crimson make purple

MIXING GOUACHE WITH WHITE

For the color wheel on the facing page, the same three colors as before are used, the yellow at the top of the wheel, blue on the left of the wheel, and crimson to the right. The only difference is that this time the paint is much thicker and, whereas before thinning the paint with water made the colors brighter, here the colors are used thickly and brightened by adding white paint.

First the adjacent colors were mixed together – without using white – and a panel painted for each new mix to form the circle. Then white was added to each panel in the circle, and new panels outside the circle created, getting progressively lighter by adding white to the color before.

The spokes inside the color wheel are made up of the three colors mixed together, to produce a strong dark color which can be adjusted to be warm or cool by adding either the warm red or the cooler blue.

Again, by experimenting you will be amazed how well these paints work together to create an astonishing spectrum of colors, and how these colors relate to each other really well because they are mixed from a limited palette.

I have used these color wheels to introduce the three colors and, in the demonstrations (see pages 38–121), will show the two completely different ways they can be used.

Panels outside the circle painted using
white added to the color in the circle
next to the panel.

White added to previous
panel

Add white to the green
to make it lighter

YELLOW OCHER

Host color

Ultramarine blue and
yellow ocher mixed
make a green

White added to host color

ULTRAMARINE
BLUE

Add white to the blue
to make it lighter

ALIZARIN CRIMSON
Color used straight from
the tube to paint the circle

USING COMPLEMENTARY COLORS

Red, yellow, and blue can be very effective when used to create complementary colors, and the color combinations are dramatic when they're placed together.

1. Here, yellow is the background color and the distant buildings are painted with its complementary color – purple – made by mixing the blue and red.

2. A red wash is used here as the background color and the distant buildings are painted with its complementary color – green – made by mixing blue and yellow.

3. This time blue is used as a background wash and the distant buildings are painted with its complementary color – orange – made by mixing red and yellow.

USING COMPLEMENTARIES TO PRODUCE GRAYS

Colors in nature are not very bright so, to ensure the colors you mix are kept subtle, use complementaries to gray them.

For example, when mixing alizarin with ultramarine to make a purple, the mixed color can look a little bright. Reduce the brightness, by adding a touch of the complementary yellow ocher, to get a more earthy gray-purple. The same applies to the other color combinations.

CREATING DEPTH

Whether you are a beginner or more experienced, to create depth
in a painting it is crucial to understand the relative shades of color.

NOTHING IS PURE WHITE

Look around you, compare the "whites" and
you'll see that they are all, in fact, different
shades. Now find a shiny object, compare the
highlighted part to the whites, and see how
much darker and more colorful the whites
appear in comparison. If this isn't understood,
and objects are painted too white and chalky,
a painting will look flat. When painting with
watered-down gouache, whites can also be
depicted by leaving an area of white paper
exposed as the highlight. For instance, sunlight
sparkling on water is dazzling white.

NOTHING IS PURE BLACK

Similarly, shadows may appear black but
reflected light will affect them, making them
different shades of dark. Look, for instance,
at a tree casting a shadow. If that shadow is
facing the sky, then the sky will reflect into
the shadow, and if the trunk is next to grass
or hay, the color of that grass or hay will be
reflected in its trunk, making it more colorful.

With the three-color palette we are using in
this book, you will see from the color wheels
on pages 23 and 25 that convincingly dark
shades can be created by mixing alizarin
crimson and ultramarine blue, and a touch
of yellow ocher.

These areas appear white on this photo, but see how much color I put in on the painting

The reflected light of this orange canopy is exaggerated on the painting

There are a lot of dark areas in the lower half of this photo. See how I dealt with them in the painting

WORK TONALLY

Don't try to match colors up exactly to nature or your photographic reference: an approximation is perfectly adequate, as it is all relative.

Know where your strongest light and dark areas will be in the scene, and work between these two parameters, painting other light areas darker than the strongest light area and the dark areas lighter than the strongest dark area.

This Moroccan street scene, in thick gouache on board, was painted from the reference photograph on the facing page. Compare the two and see how I selected the brightest area of white (in the absence of a reflective surface, the man's shirt), and I made the area on the right my strongest dark, but not black.

DARKS AND LIGHTS

Painting is a thought process. If you don't understand what's happening in the scene you will be confused and if you're confused, don't be surprised if your painting looks confused too.

Bear in mind that warm colors bring the scene forward, while cool colors recede. Look at your reference and decide where your strongest lights and darks will be. For example, in the view of Venice in the photograph (top right) the sun reflecting in the water is dazzling white, much brighter than the area of sky where the sun is, so in my painting (below right) I have made the reflection my whitest area.

The wall in the foreground (bottom right of the photograph) is the darkest area but very uninteresting and, if copied exactly in the painting, it would look too heavy. To bring the scene forward, I made the base of the first pole the darkest area, and painted the foreground wall with warm darks. Once this has been established, I know that any other area in the scene will be either darker than the light area or lighter than the dark area. Simple. If you work between these two parameters and exaggerate color effects, your paintings will have depth and drama.

The point of painting in this way is to improve on the image and make the painting more interesting and dramatic than the photograph. It is not a copying process.

In this painting the lightest part of the sky is yellow, not white, and the glow from the sun warms everything in its path. The strongest whites are in the shimmering light on the sea and the strongest darks are beneath the foreground boat. The large wave shapes in the foreground help to bring the scene forward.

Strongest whites (masked off with masking fluid and concentrated to a more clearly defined area)

Lightest part of sky is yellow, not white

Strongest darks

Note how the glow from the sun warms everything in its path

Large wave shapes in foreground, to bring the scene forward

HOW OUR EYES SEE

USING MASKING FLUID

Masking fluid can be used in watercolor-style paintings to mask off areas in the painting which have bright reflections, such as light on water, or on a shiny surface.

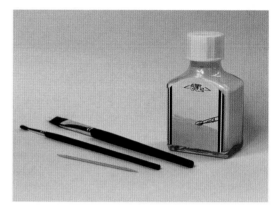

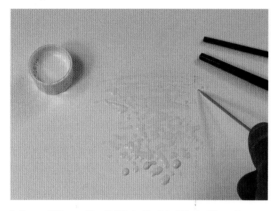

1. Pour a little masking fluid into the lid of the bottle and use the stick end of the various size brushes and cocktail sticks to create the larger blobs in the foreground and the smaller ones in the background. This will suggest distance.

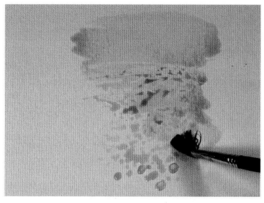

2. When dry, paint over the masking fluid, using the color to dramatize the sparkling water effect.

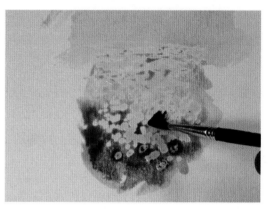

3. Do this while the washes are wet, to encourage spontaneous blending and dramatic mixing.

You will need:

- Masking fluid
- Stick end of various brushes
- Cocktail sticks

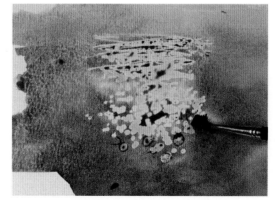

4. When the watercolor is finished allow it to dry.

5. Once the paint is dry, use a clean finger to remove the masking fluid, leaving the highlights exposed brilliant white.

LINE AND WASH

Occasionally a painting may need a line and wash treatment (*see* Mary Arden's House, page 65). A sharpened matchstick dipped in black ink gives a varied and textured line, which is very suitable for black-timbered buildings, and the effect is preferable to using a metal nib.

Dipping the sharpened matchstick into ink and using the corners, the edge, and the flat produces a variety of lines and textures.

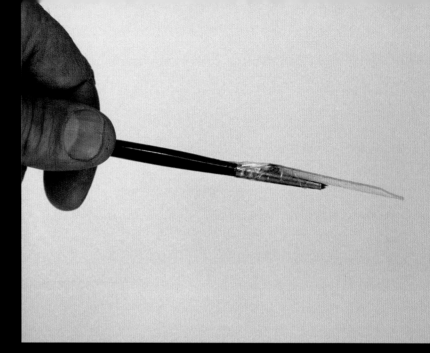

A sharpened matchstick attached with transparent adhesive tape to a discarded brush end.

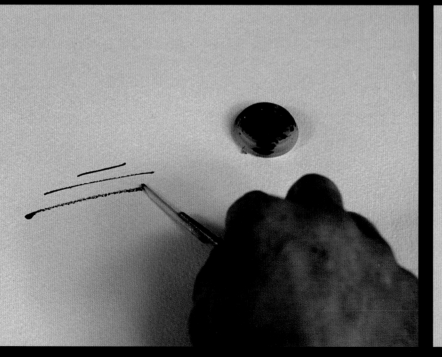

The sharpened matchstick, loaded with ink, produces fine and textured black lines.

More solid, broader textures can be achieved using the sides and flat part of the matchstick.

TACKLING SKIES

Painting skies can seem a daunting prospect and cloud formations can seem complicated (*see Eilean Donan, page 60*). Here is a way to simplify the process.

1. In this demonstration the clouds, which face the sun (top left), have been made white by painting an ocher wash and leaving the white paper exposed as the highlight.

2. Ultramarine was then mixed with a touch of alizarin and, starting at the top of the page with heavier color, the wash was diluted as it was applied down the page, painting around the cloud shapes and into the horizon.

3. Next, the blue and red were mixed to make a warm purple and then it was grayed by adding a little ocher. With this mixture the cloud shadows were painted in, darker washes for the foreground clouds, paler for the distant ones. While these washes were wet, clean water was used to soften the shadows into the rest of the clouds, making them rounder.

4. Finally, the distant hills were painted into the wet clouds.

POINTS TO REMEMBER

WHEN WORKING IN A WATERCOLOR STYLE

• Use soft-hair brushes (preferably sable) with the paint really wet. This ensures that the washes stay wet for a few minutes and, if you feel it looks wrong, you can add to the wash or lift color out with smooth bathroom tissue.

• Work light to dark, from the whites – masked-off or painted around – layering colors from yellow to light blue to a stronger blue/purple, getting progressively darker and stronger in color.

WHEN WORKING IN THICK GOUACHE STYLE

• Work dark to light on a tinted board and paint shapes in, using hog or soft-hair brushes as you see fit, bearing in mind that the tone and color will be adjusted later with specific color mixes using white.

• Don't put the white paint on the palette initially. Work the three colors as much as you can to create the image. This should look dark, as the lighter mixes will only work if the underlying color is dark enough.

WHICHEVER STYLE YOU WORK IN

• Use big brushes (it stops you putting in lots of unnecessary detail). Use the whole brush, from the side, flat, or even the wooden end to make marks. Concentrate on the big shapes that make up the scene.

• Don't throw anything away – you will learn from mistakes. Look back at work and see how you have improved and how you can make improvements in old work.

• The finished painting does not have to look like the photograph. Try and paint in the subtlety the camera has destroyed by thinking about what the light is doing to the scene, and your painting should look better than the photograph.

USING PHOTOGRAPHIC REFERENCE

• The subtlety can be missing in color photographs, as darkish tones tend to become black and light tones can bleach out to white.

• The opposite is true when working from life, when we see too much subtlety. If you stand in a field, painting for an hour, you become sensitized to the enormous subtlety in the scene around you and it can be quite bewildering.

• When working from color photographs you may find it helpful to think as if you are working from life and paint in the subtleties the camera has destroyed: in essence, when working from life think like a camera and simplify everything.

In the close ups on the facing page the same three gouache colors are used, in a watercolor style on the sailing ship (left) and in a thicker, oil-painting style on the locomotive (right). I have tried to create an impression of detail in the sailing ship, applying soft washes for the sails, using brushwork and the surface of the paper to create the textures and patterns in the sea and sky, and suggesting figures with blobs and dashes. Shapes describe the shiny surface on the boiler of the locomotive, and a pattern of shapes and tones create the illusion of detail. The marks themselves are almost abstract and by themselves mean nothing but, when seen together, they appear as a locomotive.

Painting, for me, is not about detail it's more about creating an impression using color, tone, shapes, textures and patterns to give visual clues. The viewer then uses these to fill in the details in their own minds and complete the illusion which is the subject matter.

WATERED-DOWN GOUACHE

Demonstrations

CHESTERTON WINDMILL

This scene divides nicely into quarters: the dark bottom section, the bright section above this (the sun gives the lightest area in the scene), the dramatic dark cloud next, and the blue section at the top.

METHOD

The windmill and area below it appear black, but this would look wrong in a painting, so the shadow side of the windmill has been chosen as the darkest area. All tonal values (washes) are therefore made darker than the white of the sun, or lighter than the dark in the windmill. Any area close to the sun is warmed by it, and any object facing the sun will be affected by it, so the right side of the windmill can be treated with a warm wash.

First, the photographic image is transferred to the paper (*see* Transferring the Image, pages 20–21) then, using the wide flat brush with clean water, a small circle is painted around the area of the sun and, while still wet, a pale yellow wash is added to this, working outwards from the sun and adding more yellow as we paint away from the sun and along the horizon. The yellow wash is watered out as it reaches the top section and the washes are kept wet, so they can be manipulated.

Materials Used

- Tracing-down sheet + 2H pencil
- 2 soft-hair brushes: 1 wide flat, ³⁄₈in (10mm), 1 small round No 3, with tip cut off
- Designers' gouache in alizarin crimson, ultramarine blue, and yellow ocher
- Watercolor paper
- Bathroom tissue

1. A light yellow wash isolates the lightest area (the sun), then pale, warm washes are applied to suggest a distant glow in the sky, and a pale blue wash added for the area above.

2. Stronger orange and red washes indicate the warm side of the large cloud, while purples and cool blues suggest the shadow side.

The white (brightest) area in the scene has now been isolated. When dry, the paper is again wetted around the sun and, with a stronger yellow wash, the cloud shapes are painted up to the wet sun; a little red is gradually added to the yellow, making orange, then more red is added to the mix and both sides of the sun are painted, introducing warm purples and cool blues the further out we go, to make cloud patterns. While these washes are wet, clean water is used to soften the outer edges of the clouds. The wash can then be lifted with bathroom tissue, to lighten the cloud directly above the sun [**(1)** on the previous page].

Next the middle distance and foreground clouds are painted, using an orange wash. The lighter area directly above the sun is painted first (starting with the brighter washes – it's easier to darken a wash than to lighten it). The washes are kept wet and the color is stronger than before, with red and then blue added to make purples. The clouds are cooled with more blue at the sides of the picture, and at the top of the main cloud on the shadow side. The washes in the clouds on the sides are watered away [**(2)** on the previous page].

The sky above the dark cloud is quite blue so, with ultramarine blue and a tiny bit of alizarin (the blue on its own would be too bright, the lightest part of the sky (above the sun) is painted in. A light wash is used, and the color gradually darkened as it is painted out to the edge of the paper **(3)**.

3. Stronger, warmer colors strengthen the large cloud, and more purples and blue shadow color help to bring it forward.

4. Broken cloud shapes are added to the two sides of light sky above the dark cloud, using irregular brushwork to suggest movement and drama.

When dry, some wispy clouds are indicated with textured brushwork, by skimming the surface of the paper with the flat brush. A green wash (blue and yellow) is used for this, and the color grayed – to take out the brightness – by adding a touch of red **(4)**.

The foreground is much too dark – in reality you would see the ploughed field, vegetation, and so on – so the area by the sun is wet with clean water and a warm glow from the sun is painted in, and the washes cooled as they move away from the sun **(5)**.

The paper is wet around the sun's glow, to exaggerate it with oranges and browns (made by adding blue to the orange), and some purples are painted in further away from the sun. When dry, the small brush is used to paint in the windmill: warm reds for the sunny side and cooler color for the left, darker shadow side. The top of the windmill is then painted, noting the blue reflected light from the sky, then the sails are painted in a warm, light color for those near the sun, and a slightly darker color for the others. Before they dry, the stick end of the brush is used to push the wet paint out from the sail, to give detail. Now, when dry, we return to the windmill and, starting at the darkest area – the shadow side of the windmill – a darker bluey-purple is used and the color watered into the previous wash. It is lightened slightly and some foreground textures are painted in the earth.

If required, the areas of the clouds catching the sun can be warmed up and the shadow side darkened **(6)**.

5. The warm washes emanating from the sun become cooler at the sides, so completing the lower part of the painting.

6. Warm washes are applied to the right side of the windmill and the landscape below it, describing the sun's influence, while cool washes are used on the left side of the windmill, which is cast into shadow. Textured brushwork adds interest to the landscape.

NOON, VENICE

Here the sun, high in the sky, is reflected in the sparkle in the water, and this will be the lightest area in the painting. The darkest area is the top of the first pole in the foreground. The silhouette of the church gives distance, the boat and jetty on the left are the middle distance, while the three poles are the foreground.

METHOD

First, the photographic image is transferred to the paper (*see* Transferring the Image, pages 20-21). Then, using the stick ends of the brushes, masking fluid is applied to the highlighted areas (*see* Using Masking Fluid, on page 33). This makes interesting patterns: small blobs in the distance, which spread into horizontal streaks, and large individual blobs in the foreground. Then, a cocktail stick is used to mask out the tiny highlights on the tops of the poles facing the sun.

Once dry, a yellow ocher wash is painted with the large brush over the whole sheet, starting with a pale yellow where the sun was in the sky and radiating out from there, to cover the sheet with slightly heavier yellow around the sparkle. While the washes are wet, a light wash of alizarin crimson is added in the foreground and pale orange color further back.

Materials Used

- Tracing-down sheet + 2H pencil
- Masking fluid
- Cocktail stick
- 2 soft-hair brushes: 1 large flat, ½in (12mm), 1 small round No 3, with tip cut off
- Designers' gouache: alizarin crimson, ultramarine blue, and yellow ocher
- Watercolor paper
- Bathroom tissue

1. Using the stick ends of the brushes and a cocktail stick, masking fluid is applied to the paper to highlight the lightest areas. Yellow ocher and pale blue washes are painted over the whole sheet.

2. Working fast with wet, pale washes, the silhouette of the distant buildings is painted in.

3. The pattern is blocked in with warm and cool tones for the poles and boat, and gaps are left to suggest highlights on the edges of the boat facing the sky.

4. Wave shapes are suggested, larger in the foreground and smaller in the distance, then the poles are painted in with stronger and warmer tones in front, paler tones as they recede.

When dry, the area around the sun is wetted with clean water, and ultramarine with a touch of alizarin is applied in a very pale blue wash. This radiates out from the wet circle to the edges of the paper, making the sky color slightly darker at the top and paler towards the horizon. Some of the pale blue wash around the sparkle is lifted out with bathroom tissue **[(1)** on previous page].

When dry, the silhouette of the church is painted in one wet wash. An orange wash is mixed for the top side of the large dome, which faces the sun; then the color is adjusted and a light bluey-purple is mixed and painted in the cooler shadow side; the tones are allowed to blend together and the paint pushed out with the stick end of the brush, to give the statue shape on top. The paint is left wet, so the colors blend. More blue is added to the top of the main dome (where the sky is reflected), then with a clean brush yellow is added to the top right section on the main dome, and some color lifted out to lighten the curve facing the sun.

The rest of the silhouette is painted and the shapes are cooled and darkened as appropriate: the other domes are painted paler blue to suggest distance and the section above the sparkle is kept light and warm to suggest reflected light off the sparkle. The whole shape is filled in and, before the wash dries, the bottom edge is watered away so the buildings fade into the water **(2)**.

Next, the middle distance: the jetty is painted in as are the boat and reflections – detail is not important, this painting is about mood – cool colors to the left, warmer to the right, facing the light. When dry, the poles are painted in with a small brush; they are rearranged as necessary, using cooler colors away from the light and warmer on the right. Then, starting at the bottom of the sheet, the stylized wave shapes are painted in with the wide flat brush – larger in the foreground, smaller further back – and the shapes watered out with clean water as they recede and are affected by the sparkle **(3)**.

Using a small brush and a purple mix (blue and a touch of alizarin), the top of the first pole is painted in and, as it reaches the sparkle, the wash is warmed up with orange, and the rest of the pole and the reflection are painted in. The second pole is painted with slightly paler (watered-down) color, but this time the left (shadow) side is painted with the purple mix and the right side (facing the light) with orange. The third pole is purple all over but some color is lifted off with bathroom tissue, to lighten the base slightly. Next, the red stripes on the poles are painted in with one brush mark using the small brush – flattened out to the correct width – and the color is adjusted to orange at the base **(4)**.

5. Finally, the top of the front pole is darkened and, when the paint is dry, the masking fluid is removed.

We started with the white highlights using masking fluid, and progressed with pale cool colors in the distance, painting stronger, warmer colors as we came forward. Now the darkest area at the top of the first pole is painted, the stripes with a stronger warm shadowy red, the colors on the poles adjusted as appropriate, and some suggested detail in the middle ground is painted with pale dark washes. When dry, a clean finger is used to rub away the masking fluid and the painting is finished **(5)**.

FULL SAIL

Although the reference photograph (right) is dull, it does suggest light coming from the top left, highlighting the front part of the sails (the lightest areas in the scene). The strongest dark area is the bow of the ship.

METHOD

A quick pencil sketch explores the tonal patterns: dark sky against light sail, darker sail against lighter sky. With a little artistic license – the sky and clouds are treated as a collection of shapes – textures and tones are used to highlight the ship and give the scene some drama. Light comes from the top left, so the clouds will be highlighted on the top left sides, making their shadow sides bottom right **(1)**.

A yellow-ocher wash is applied with the large brush, and the white areas on the front edges of the sails are isolated by painting around the highlights and softening the wash in the sail. When dry, the sky is painted in, using ultramarine with a touch of alizarin crimson: stronger washes are applied at the top, paler as the sky meets the horizon to give the sky depth. The ocher wash is left exposed as cloud color. Some washes are softened on the underside of the cloud shapes with clean water **(2)**.

Materials Used

• 2 soft-hair brushes: 1 large flat, ½in (12mm), 1 small round No 3, with tip cut off
• Designers' gouache in alizarin crimson, ultramarine blue, and yellow ocher
• Watercolor paper
• 4B pencil
• Ruler
• Bathroom tissue

1. A quick freehand sketch shows the tonal values of light against dark, and dark against light.

2. The tonal patterns are established with pale washes, isolating the white areas (the front edges of the sails) by painting around them.

3. Soft washes are used to indicate the lights and darks in the sails, the land and the water are blocked in, and the cloud shapes strengthened.

4. The wave shapes and details on the sails and boat are painted in, and more color wash is applied in the sky.

5. By building up the washes in layers – paler in the distance, bolder in the foreground – more control is given:
a pale wash can be darkened easily by painting over it again, but a dark wash, once dry, cannot be lightened easily.

Next, the shadow side of the sails is painted in, softening the washes, and the land indicated with a purple wash and a touch of ocher (this tones down the purple, if it's too bright on its own). The edges of the land mass are softened with clean water, to blur the land into the distance. A pale green is mixed and the sea painted in, with a wash slightly darker in the foreground and paler in the distance. The ship's hull is painted in purple with a touch of ocher, the masts are indicated with brushruling (*see page 17*) and the deck with brown washes (mixed from orange and ultramarine). The sky is warmed up on the horizon on the left and cloud shapes are painted in with purple grays, using texture and soft washes **(3)**.

The shadow sides of the sails are darkened, figures and more detail on the deck indicated; then some interesting patterns in the sea, suggesting waves, are painted in with the purple-gray used in the sky **(4)**.

All the tonal patterns are now in place, so the clouds, waves, and sails are refined. Using a small brush, more detail is painted in on the ship: the hull is darkened at the front and made lighter towards the stern, and flags and other detail in the sails are put in. When dry, a soft pencil and ruler are used to draw in some of the ropes **(5)**.

SILVERY LIGHT, ST IVES

Here, the sun is directly above the sparkling water (lightest area) backlighting the boats and buildings, apart from some of the roofs angled just right to catch the sunlight. The landscape behind the church fades away into the distance with cool blues, while the strong darks in the foreground boat bring it forward, as will the red buoys hanging off the side.

METHOD

First, the photographic image is traced off (*see* Transferring the Image, pages 20–21). Then, using masking fluid and the stick ends of the brushes the sparkling light is blanked out (*see* Using Masking Fluid, page 33). Larger shapes are made in the foreground, smaller shapes in the distance, creating interesting patterns to give the water some movement. When dry, the whole sheet is washed over with a yellow-ocher wash **(1)**.

When the yellow wash is dry, the sky area where the sun will be is wetted with clean water, and a pale blue wash (ultramarine and a touch of alizarin) introduced to the wet patch, leaving some of the yellow ocher exposed. The roof shapes catching the light are painted around and the tones kept pale (watery) around the sparkle.

Materials Used

- Tracing-down sheet + 2H pencil
- Masking fluid
- 2 soft-hair brushes: 1 large flat, 1/2in (12mm), 1 small round No 3, with tip cut off
- Designers' gouache: alizarin crimson, ultramarine blue, and yellow ocher
- Watercolor paper
- Bathroom tissue

1. Masking fluid – used to blank out some areas – establishes an interesting pattern of sunlight reflecting in the water, then a pale yellow wash (representing sunlight) is washed over the whole sheet.

2. Blue washes are used to highlight the roof shapes. Some highlights are yellow and some pale blue, but white is not used.

3. The shapes of distant buildings are suggested and brought forward with warmer washes where they catch the sun's warmth and reflected light off the sparkling water.

A purple-blue is used to paint in the distant landscape, around more roof shapes, and the same wash used to indicate a few larger wave shapes in the foreground, watering them out, smaller and paler as they recede **(2)**.

The distant, cool building shapes are painted in, suggesting variety. Coming forward in the scene, the church and other buildings are painted in, their color warming slightly as they catch the sun directly and are lit up by the reflected light of the sparkle in the water. Not much detail is needed **(3)**.

Using pale washes, the distant boats are painted in as silhouettes and warmed slightly as they sit on the sparkling water **(4)**.

Finally, the foreground boats are painted in, suggesting some detail, the sides facing the light highlighted, and the front boat's hull is warmed with reflected light off the red buoys **(5)**.

4. Wet washes are used, in progressively stronger tones, to block in the silhouettes of the distant boat shapes.

5. To ensure that the edges are crisper and that more detail is shown, the paler washes are allowed to dry before the main boat shapes are blocked in.

6. With a small brush, stronger, darker color is used to add foreground detail, then paler dark color is used for items further back in the scene.

Up to now the white areas and pale washes have been progressively darkened as we came forward in the scene, giving an impression of depth. Now a small brush is used and, starting with the strongest darks in the hull of the foreground boat, detail is painted in where appropriate, warming the tones where necessary and adjusting the colors on the buoys. The tonal values on the boat behind are strengthened as necessary and enough detail is picked out to bring the boat forward, so that – tonally – it sits comfortably against the boat in front (it's much too dark in the photo). Water movement lines are painted around the boats in the foreground, and detail is just suggested in the boats behind (the foreground boats are the focal point and more detail in the background would detract from them). When dry, the masking fluid is rubbed away with a clean finger **(6)**.

WILLY LOTT'S COTTAGE

There is no direct sunlight in this scene (right), but the lightest part is the patch of sky behind the roof and the strongest darks are in the foreground trees on the right side. Remember dark objects (the roofs and trees) reflect lighter in water, while light objects (the white walls) reflect darker.

METHOD

First, the photographic image is traced off
(*see* Transferring the Image, pages 20-21). Then,
using the wide brush, a yellow wash is painted
over the whole sheet, apart from the white area
in the sky behind the cottage roof, where the
wash is softened to pure white. When dry, the
sky is painted in with ultramarine and a touch of
alizarin, darker at the top and paler lower down,
leaving a few gaps in the sky to allow the yellow
clouds to show. The reflection of the sky in the
water is painted a tone darker than the sky.
Warm, pale washes are used to begin to suggest
the walls of the building **(1)**.

The building and tree shapes are blocked in
with pale washes. Greens are mixed by adding
varying amounts of blue to the yellow and
the color is adjusted by adding more yellow,
or water, for a brighter green, more blue for
a darker green, and a touch of red to gray
the greens.

Materials Used

- Tracing-down sheet + 2H pencil
- 2 soft-hair brushes: 1 large flat, ½in
  (12mm), 1 small round No 3, with tip cut off
- Designers' gouache: alizarin crimson,
  ultramarine blue, and yellow ocher
- Watercolor paper
- Bathroom tissue

1. Pale washes are used to establish the lightest area in the painting and pale color is used to indicate the sky, water, and building.

2. Light washes are added to indicate the individual tree shapes and the roof.

3. Reflections are added, with large washes and broken shapes to suggest movement in the water.

4. More definition is added to the trees, allowing the previous pale washes to show as highlights facing the patch of light in the sky.

The individual tree shapes are described with appropriate color: cool blues, purples, and browns are used in shadow areas, texture is used to suggest leaves (some bushes appear orange), and the light walls are reflected dark in the water **(2)**.

The foliage in the foreground is painted with texture and washes, and the reflections of the trees and cottage roof and windows are blocked in. The colors are adjusted as necessary and the corner of the brush is used to leave gaps to suggest movement in the water breaking up the reflections **(3)**.

More definite tree shapes are painted in, using texture and a variety of colors to suggest individual trees **(4)**.

Darker purple-based washes painted over the tree shapes help to unite the trees as a mass, and to contrast more against the lighter trees. The shadow tones now suggest the individual tree shapes with a little more subtlety.

5. The reflection of the sky and the movement shapes in the water are strengthened.

The roof color on the house is painted in, window shapes and more plants are suggested in front of the cottage to bring the scene forward, and more shadow areas blocked in the trees, keeping the distant ones pale. The lights in the scene are exaggerated with textured brush marks to make it more interesting and the greens changed by adding more yellow, blue, and red to the mixes. Light patches are left in the trees to suggest tree trunks, branches, and fencing. The water is darkened in the foreground, with a big wash breaking the shape up to suggest movement lines in the water **(5)**.

Color is added to the trees on the right and the dark color brought down slightly paler into the water, suggesting some movement in the shadows. Any foreground trees are painted over and shadows and shapes strengthened. The shadow side of the chimney is painted in to contrast against the light sky and a shadow painted in across the gravel drive on the left **(6)**.

6. Darker washes are painted over the tree shapes, so they blend together more, and the trees on the right are darkened.

EILEAN DONAN CASTLE

In this scene, I liked the simplicity of the castle silhouetted against the distant hills, and the way the hills merge into the sky. The whitest area is the sun shimmering in the water and the strongest darks are in the foreground rocks.

METHOD

First, the photographic image is traced off (*see* Transferring the Image, pages 20-21). The sun is above the clouds to the left of the castle, reflecting in the shimmer directly below. This area of pure white is masked off using masking fluid applied with the stick end of a small paintbrush (*see* Using Masking Fluid, page 33).

Once the masking fluid has dried, the large brush is used to apply a pale yellow tone over the whole sheet. When dry, blue with a touch of crimson is painted in the sky area, working from the tops of the cloud shapes, and making the blue paler as it gets nearer the horizon. While still wet, a little more crimson and ocher are added to the blue and the shadow patterns of the clouds painted in, darker at the top, paler as they come nearer the horizon. The patterns are washed and blended together to make an interesting pattern in the sky and, while still wet, the distant hills are washed in **(1)**.

Materials Used

- Tracing-down sheet + 2H pencil
- Masking fluid
- 2 soft-hair brushes: 1 large flat, ½in (12mm), 1 small round No 3, with tip cut off
- Designers' gouache: alizarin crimson, ultramarine blue, and yellow ocher
- Watercolor paper
- Bathroom tissue

1. Masking fluid protects the white areas, while the yellow wash – which will give the highlights in the clouds – is painted around with sky and cloud tones.

2. The distant hills and water are suggested with pale washes.

3. More definite hill shapes are added on the left and the beach area is blocked in with pale washes.

Next, the water is painted in with blue and a touch of crimson a tone darker than the sky. Starting at the front, the water is painted along the shore, then the color is thinned to make the wash paler as it recedes. The color is washed away with clean water when it reaches the horizon, so it blends with the other dry washes.

The now-dry distant hills are wetted with clean water and the hills washed in on the right. They are kept fuzzy in the distance and crisper as they come closer and the edges of the hill lifted with bathroom tissue to make the edge crisp. With clean water the bottom edge of the hill is washed away **(2)**.

The hills on the left are painted next, with a slightly stronger tone on the left, paler as they recede and the bottom edge softened slightly where the hill meets the water. The bottom right corner of the scene is filled with warmer washes, suggesting the underlying colors in the foreground.

4. Warm brown seaweed and exaggerated wave shapes are indicated.

A careful look at this area on the photograph will reveal hints of color there – this is used as a guide only and no attempt is made to match any particular color. Now the sheet is covered with approximate color and, working tonally, the washes are made progressively darker and warmer as we come forward in the scene **(3)**.

Next, some wave shapes are painted in and the size of the shapes exaggerated: larger in the foreground and smaller and paler as they go back. The brown-colored seaweed is added and some shale and rock shapes start to be indicated, as well as grasses and shrubbery. Using a small brush the castle is now painted with shadowy blue washes, not too dark, greens are added by the castle and then, moving on, a little detail is suggested in the hills on the left **(4)**.

Starting with the strongest darks, the shadow sides of the foreground rocks are indicated, becoming paler as they recede – and the browns and greens are strengthened in color and texture. This helps to bring the scene forward and contrasts the strong, dark, warm textures against the cooler, paler washes in the background. When dry, the masking fluid is removed with a clean finger **(5)**.

5. The castle is painted in and the foreground rocks are suggested by a pattern of shapes and textures.

MARY ARDEN'S HOUSE

In the photograph (right) the sun is in the top left hand side of the scene, casting long shadows over the whitewashed walls, which are the white areas in the scene. The darks in the painting will be the beams on the shadow side of the building on the right.

1. Black Indian ink, applied with a sharpened matchstick, is used to draw in the darkest areas in the scene.

Materials Used

- Tracing-down sheet + 2H pencil
- A sharpened matchstick
- Black Indian waterproof ink
- 2 soft-hair brushes: 1 large flat, ½in (12mm), 1 small round No 3, with tip cut off
- Designers' gouache: alizarin crimson, ultramarine blue, and yellow ocher
- Watercolor paper

METHOD

First the photographic image is traced off (*see* Transferring the Image, pages 20-21). Then, with a sharpened matchstick dipped in the black ink, the dark shadowed areas are drawn in with loaded ink, to give a solid black line. Then, with the nib not as fully loaded and the ink used more sparingly, the textures in the dark woodwork are suggested (*see* Line and Wash, page 34). On the shadow side, some areas are treated more solidly and other areas have more texture – the drawing does not need to look too heavy **(1)**.

This time no overall yellow wash is used, as the white areas in the building will be painted around. The buildings will provide whites in the scene, while the black ink has already established the dark areas.

The sky section is covered in a yellow ocher wash – slightly stronger at the top and paler as it reaches the horizon – and painted into the roof area but not the walls of the building. While this is wet, the streaks of blue with a touch of crimson are painted in – darker at the top and paler, more watered down, at the horizon.

2. The streaky sky is painted in, and pale purple-gray washes are used to describe the wooden beam patterns, walls, and road. Warm washes indicate the courtyard.

Next, the yellow and orange area behind the gate is painted. As it comes forward onto the pavement, more red is added to the orange and then blue is added to the mix for the road area. Once this is dry, the windows, walls, and beams are painted in, noting the changes in color on the beams **(2)**.

The shadows on the building and walls are painted next, including the reflected orange color in the shadow on the wall. Then the roof is indicated with a light wash of yellow and red, and, when dry, a brown wash – made from yellow, red, and blue – is painted on, but the previous wash is allowed to show through, to suggest tiles. Pale purple washes block in the distant buildings **(3)**.

The trees and hedges come next, the pale yellows put in first and color built up, using the texture of the paper to suggest leaves. The wall and hedge on the right are darkened with purples and greens, which are allowed to fuse. Finally, shadows are added to the foreground, stronger in the foreground, paler as they recede **(4)**.

3. Roofs are indicated – paler in the distance, more solidly and warmer in the foreground – and the shadow shapes are blocked in.

4. Pale yellow-green color indicates the highlights in the hedges, darker greens and browns describe the shadows. The woodwork pattern is developed further with brown washes.

BLUE LAGOON

In this early-morning view of Venice there is no direct sunlight, only lamps reflecting in the canal. These will give us the lightest area in the painting, while the darkest area will be the base of the front pole.

1. To set the mood in the scene, a wash of blue with a touch of crimson is painted over a dry, pale-yellow wash.

Materials Used

- Tracing-down sheet + 2H pencil
- Masking fluid
- 2 soft-hair brushes: 1 large flat, ½in (12mm), 1 small round No 3, with tip cut off
- Designers' gouache: alizarin crimson, ultramarine blue, yellow ocher
- Watercolor paper
- Bathroom tissue
- Ruler

METHOD

First the photographic image is traced off (see Transferring the Image, pages 20–21). Then masking fluid is applied to the lamp areas and reflection (see Using Masking Fluid, page 33). When dry, the large flat brush is used to apply a pale yellow wash over the whole sheet. When this dries, ultramarine with a touch of crimson is used to paint a wash slightly darker at the top, paler towards the horizon and, from the horizon towards the bottom of the page, a tone darker than at the top of the sky. (Skies are darker blue above our heads and paler on the horizon, and water reflects sky at least a tone darker, so the water at our feet is darker, and paler as it recedes toward the horizon.)

There are no bright colors in this scene, so a touch of the complementary yellow is added to a purple mixed from blue and crimson, to achieve some more suitable gray mixes. The colors do not match the reference. An approximate value is all that's necessary, keeping the distance cool and pale and the foreground darker and slightly warmer **(1)**.

2. Working around the boat and pole shapes, the pattern of the building shapes is painted in, softening the bottom edges into the canal.

3. As the building shapes come forward, the color becomes slightly warmer.

4. The landscape on the left is blocked in, together with the main shapes in the boats, buildings, and pavement area.

5. The pole shapes and reflections are indicated and horizontal brushwork is added to suggest the canal in the foreground.

Next, the distant buildings are painted in with bluey-purples, working around the boat shapes and poles. The color for the main dome is cooled with blue and the shapes watered out to suggest the roundness, then the color is warmed with crimson and ocher as the buildings come forward. While the washes are wet the edge of the buildings is softened where they meet the water **(2 and 3)**.

The wall on the right is washed in and the pavement is suggested. The buildings and boats are painted in as simple shapes on the left. A dull brown mix is used for the distant poles, warming up slightly as the poles come forward.

6. The lamps, foreground walls, and pavement are indicated. Window features are suggested with pale washes on the distant buildings and some streaks are added to describe the water movement.

7. The strong darks are painted in at the base of the front pole and the red stripes strengthened. With paler darks, some detail is added in the boats and pavement, where necessary.

The red stripes are indicated on the poles in front and some wave shapes suggested in the foreground, and faded away as they recede **(4 and 5)**.

The detail in the buildings on the right is painted in, the colors are warmed up with red and ocher but kept quite shadowy with blue. The pavement edge and the main poles are defined, and some movement lines in the water indicated **(6)**.

The base of the front pole is redefined with the small brush, using a strong dark red for the stripes and paler washes used to do the same for the other poles. The perspective lines on the pavement are brushruled (see Brushruling, page 17), breaking the lines up with gaps. Some pale darks are touched in where necessary on the building on the right, with even paler, cooler washes indicated on some windows on the buildings further back on the right, and some detail in the boats is suggested. When dry, the masking fluid is removed with a clean finger and, using a very pale wash, some yellow reflections are spotted in the water and the distant lamps **(7)**.

LADIES' VIEW, KILLARNEY

The meandering lakes connect the cool blues in the distant hills and the warm browns in the foreground. The light comes from directly above: the water will be the white area in the painting and the strongest dark area will be in the large foreground rock.

1. Working from the whites towards the darks, the white areas of the lakes are isolated with an ocher wash, which becomes very pale for the cloud area.

Materials Used

• Tracing-down sheet + 2H pencil
• 2 soft-hair brushes: 1 large flat, $\frac{1}{2}$in (12mm), 1 small round No 3, with tip cut off
• Designers' gouache: alizarin crimson, ultramarine blue, yellow ocher
• Watercolor paper
• Bathroom tissue

METHOD

First the photographic image is traced off (*see* Transferring the Image, pages 20-21). Next, the wide brush is used to cover the paper with a thin wash of yellow ocher, kept very pale in the cloud area, a little heavier around the lakes. The lake shapes are exposed as white paper (masking fluid isn't used, as it leaves a very hard edge). When dry, the sky is painted in using ultramarine with a touch of crimson and, softening the washes with clean water, a touch of ocher is added to the mixture in the gray undersides of the clouds and the edges softened, as appropriate. The cloud shapes are not distinct in the reference but we know the light is coming from above. The clouds are made by painting up to the top edge with sky color, highlighting the top of the cloud shape, and painting the shadow side with a purple-gray. The shadow wash is softened towards the top of the cloud shape, to give the cloud a rounded appearance **(1)**. (*See* Tackling Skies , page 35.)

2. The sky, cloud shapes, and distant hills are blocked in and the landscape warmed with stronger washes as it comes forward.

3. The right-hand hills are blocked in using cool and warm washes and, while the wash is slightly wet, the blurred shapes are painted in. The warm tones around the winding lakes are strengthened.

The very distant blue hills are painted in with a cool wash and watered out into the distance with clean water. The rest of the hills are painted in, first with an orange wash (ocher with a touch of crimson), then blues and purples are added to the damp wash to suggest distant blurred trees, and the tops of the hills watered away on the left and right **(2 and 3)**.

The warm orange washes are continued, to highlight the lakes and block in the rocks and vegetation with washes and textures **(4)**.

Starting towards the back of the scene and using textured strokes, the middle distance is blocked in. If the washes look too dark in the distance, they are lifted out and softened with bathroom tissue, before they dry.

4. A pale gray tone indicates the rocks in the foreground, then darker, textured strokes are placed on top to suggest the rugged nature of the rocks. Warmer brown tones are added to indicate grasses.

5. With progressively darker and warmer washes, the main patterns of the trees and landscape are blocked in and texture is used to suggest detail.

The texture of the paper is used to create interesting shapes and patterns, and the colors are warmed as they come forward **(5)**.

With a small brush, the foreground rock is darkened on the left side, leaving gaps to highlight grasses and using texture to describe the rock surface. The grasses are painted in and the color adjusted as required; going back into the scene, the rock shapes, tree trunks, trees, and bushes are suggested and, with a pale gray, the shadow sides to the edges of the lakes are painted in. There is no need for too much detail, as the soft washes in the background, contrasting against the textured brushwork in the foreground, suggest the detail.

This scene is painted in quite an abstract process – a collection of washes, textures and blobs that in themselves seem meaningless but, when seen together, make up an evocative landscape **(6)**.

6. More dark and warm tones are added to bring the scene forward, with a pattern of grasses, rocks, and textures contrasting against the softer and paler distant shapes.

MORNING LIGHT

In this view of San Giorgio Maggiore, Venice, the reflected sun in the canal gives the strongest white in the scene and the strongest darks will be in the foreground boat. There is a cool, pale slither of landscape in the distance and the main buildings are backlit in the middle ground, leaving the boat nicely in the foreground.

METHOD

First, the photographic image is traced off (see Transferring the Image, pages 20-21). Then the reflected light is masked off with masking fluid, using the stick ends of the brushes (see Using Masking Fluid, page 33). Large blobs are applied in the foreground, smaller blobs and streaks in the background, creating interesting shapes and patterns in the process. When dry, the wide, flat brush is used to paint over the whole sheet with a wash of yellow ocher, then left to dry **(1)**.

Next, a stronger yellow wash is applied from the top and painted over the sky area, crimson is added to make orange, then more red and finally blue is added to the palette to make a purple. The color is kept brighter in the area of sky where the sun is, and slightly darker further away. The cooler washes are brought down towards the bottom of the sheet, leaving a few gaps showing the previous wash to suggest waves catching the light. The bottom-left reflections warmed up with a light red wash **(2)**.

Materials Used

- Tracing-down sheet + 2H pencil
- 2 soft-hair brushes: 1 large flat, ½in (12mm), 1 small round No 3, with tip cut off
- Designers' gouache: alizarin crimson, ultramarine blue, yellow ocher
- Watercolor paper
- Bathroom tissue

1. Working light to dark, the white areas are masked off and an ocher wash painted over the whole sheet.

2. While keeping washes brighter in the area where the sun is in the sky, warmer washes are added to the sky and water to set the mood.

3. Starting with the background, progressively stronger washes are applied to the buildings, while the paler
tones on the left suggest reflected light off the shimmering water.

4. The main shapes of the boat are painted in, suggesting reflected light warming up the stern. A pattern of exaggerated wave shapes is indicated.

5. A dark tone is mixed and, working from the darkest area towards the light, the bow is painted in with a strong shadow color and a paler wash is used to suggest some detail in the boat on the shadow side.

When the red wash is dry, the distant land mass is painted in and faded off with clean water into the distance. Next, the shapes of the tower are painted in using a warm purple mix, as suggested in the photograph. The slight color changes in the buildings are noted, and the color kept paler near the light, to suggest light reflecting into those buildings, and cooler on the right-hand side away from the light. Before the washes dry, the bottom edge of the buildings is watered away and made to fade into the canal **(3)**.

Next, some wave shapes are painted in the foreground, slightly darker and larger in the front, smaller and paler as they go back. When dry, the boat is painted in using warm washes to suggest the light catching the stern of the boat and to indicate the cabin and the figure **(4)**.

With a small brush, the shadow side at the front of the boat is now painted in and the wash watered out into the rest of the boat, to suggest the shadow side of the cabin and any other detail. If at this stage the painting looks a little pale in any area, a wash can be carefully applied to deepen the colors, but care should be taken to avoid disturbing the dry washes underneath. When dry, the masking fluid is removed with a clean finger **(5)**.

THICK
GOUACHE

Demonstrations

ST MARK'S BASILICA
IN THE SNOW

There is no direct sunlight in this photograph of the basilica in Venice (right), but what there is catches the snow on the domes, and these will be the lightest part of the painting. The strongest darks will be in the small figures in the distance.

METHOD

First, the photographic image is traced off (*see Transferring the Image, pages 20–21*). Then the large soft-hair brush is used to paint a yellow ocher wash over the whole sheet, apart from the white areas in the domes and tops of the buildings. The tops of the domes are given crisp edges but the color inside them is softened by watering the washes out, to give them a rounded appearance. (The sky is blue in the photographic reference, but I chose a yellow sky to contrast against the purple-gray basilica and to brighten the scene.) The top part of the basilica is blocked in with some detail, using light purple and ocher washes, so that the spires, domes, and statues contrast nicely against the lighter sky **(1)**.

Next, the remainder of the basilica, the tower and buildings are blocked in, continuing the purple washes into the square **(2)**.

Materials Used
- Tracing-down sheet + 2H pencil
- 2 soft-hair brushes: 1 large flat, ½in (12mm), 1 small round No 3, with tip cut off
- 2 bristle brushes: 1 wide flat in (10mm), 1 small flat in (6mm), or less
- Designers' gouache: alizarin crimson, ultramarine blue, yellow ocher and permanent white
- Watercolor paper
- Bathroom tissue
- Ruler

1. First, thin washes are used in a watercolor style: a yellow wash highlights the white areas of snow on the domes, and purple-gray washes describe the domed curves.

2. Big washes block in the main shapes of the building, square, and tower.

3. More washes indicate the shapes of arches and columns, exaggerating the colors suggested in the photograph.

4. With a small brush and ruler, the flagpoles and other details are suggested and the textured snow is blocked in using permanent white.

5. Starting with the strong darks in the figures, paler darks are used to focus some of the detail in the basilica as necessary.

The larger shapes in the basilica are indicated, the colors used on the building mixed together to keep them gray and stop the palette becoming too clean and bright **(3)**.

More detail is painted in using the smaller, soft-haired brush and colors kept pale and gray, resisting the temptation to paint in strong darks in the main doorway. The flagpoles and the stripes in the tower are painted in with a brown tint, then the small figures using a stronger tint. Next, some permanent white is put out on a spare saucer and, using the larger bristle brush, a touch of blue is added to the white. This paint – used straight out of the tube without adding water – should have a creamy texture but, if it is a little dry, a tiny amount of water can be added to moisten it. The background snow is painted in with this mixture, the paint smoothed out, becoming bolder with the shapes and textures in the foreground and allowing the underlying washes to show through the gaps and give color and texture to the foreground. A little blue and crimson is added to the white and with the smaller bristle brush, some marks are made to suggest footprints **(4)**.

When the white areas are dry the original palette is returned to and, with the small soft-haired brush, the three small figures are painted in the strongest darks. The dark mixture is watered down and, with the color adjusted as necessary, some detail in the basilica is flicked in as appropriate, being careful not to make the detail too dark and lose the pale, distant feel of the building **(5)**.

GOLDEN
RETRIEVER

There is no strong sunlight in the photograph (above) and what light there is comes from the top, so the lightest area is the top of the dog's head and the darkest area is on the underside of her mouth. However, for the painting, the eye shadows have been chosen as the strongest dark, as the eyes are more interesting.

METHOD

An illustration technique is used here; this
is a great way to paint an accurate likeness,
whatever the subject.

First, the image is traced off (*see Transferring
the Image*, pages 20–21). Using the soft, 4B
pencil, the dark features and shapes in the
face are drawn in, shading in some of the areas.
Then, with a yellow-ocher wash and the large
soft brush, a wash is painted over the whole
area, including over the edges, to fix the
pencil and paint out all the white areas **(1)**.

Materials Used

- Tracing-down sheet + hard (2H) pencil
- 2 soft-hair brushes: 1 wide, flat ½in
  (12mm), 1 small round, size 3, with the
  tip cut off
- Designers' gouache: alizarin crimson,
  ultramarine blue, yellow ocher and
  permanent white
- Tracedown sheet (see pages 18–19)
- Soft pencil (4B)
- Watercolor board
- Bathroom tissue

1. The dark areas are drawn in with the soft pencil, using heavier pencil marks and shading as appropriate.

2. Pale washes are used to describe the main features in the retriever's face.

3. Working from the chosen dark area (the eyes), the paler darks are indicated and used to add more detail to the features in the face.

4. As the dark washes become paler and browner, they are used to describe shapes made by the fur on the face and the body. Green and blue washes highlight the top and side of the face.

Next, the large brush is used with an orange wash (ocher and crimson mixed) to paint in the main shadow shapes in the lightest areas. The mixture is then warmed with more crimson and the nose area painted in, and a touch of blue added for the tongue and inside the mouth **(2)**.

The small round brush is used to mix a dark shade from ultramarine blue and alizarin crimson and, starting with the darkest area, the eye shapes are painted in; then, making the color slightly paler with water, the area under the nose, warming the mixture with crimson for the shapes inside the mouth, and filling in the dark areas in the eyes and mouth with cool purple/blue washes **(3)**.

The shapes in the ears are painted in with warm browns and the tones in the patterns around the head adjusted with blue paint. To highlight the top of the head, a shape is painted in behind with a green mix; a little crimson is added and this tone applied to the right-hand part of that shape to darken it. For variety and to suggest the cooler shadow side, a blue wash is added behind the ear, then watered out to soften the shapes in the background. No tone is painted around the darker nose and mouth area **(4)**.

Where necessary, the colors are strengthened: the shapes in the nose are described and honed and texture is added under the nose and mouth; the shadows in the eyes, nose, and mouth are darkened **(5)**.

Some white gouache is put out on a spare saucer and a touch of yellow ocher added to make it less bright. Then, using the paint straight out of the tube, some textures are painted in on the top of the head and ear with a small brush, and more yellow and a hint of blue added for the areas in the cheek and below the ear and teeth (the lights get darker as they face away from the light). A touch of purple is added to the white and the highlights in the eye and mouth are painted in, then, with almost a pure white, some whiskers, eyebrows, and ear fur are flicked in. Lastly the light area in front of the mouth is painted in using an almost pure white (a touch of water is added if it is too thick) and the shapes are sharpened, to give a strong contrast **(6)**.

5. Slightly darker and more precise brushwork describes and clarifies the shapes in the face.

6. White with a touch of ocher is used to highlight the top of the dog's head, and to indicate the straggly hairs and fur texture on the body.

SHIMMERING LIGHT

In this photograph of Venice (right), the sun is high in the sky on the left side and reflecting nicely in the canal, giving us the strong whites. The strongest darks are in the front part of the gondola, away from the shimmer.

1. Working from dark to light, a strong, dark mixture is used to block in the gondola and boat behind. A touch of white is then added to the palette and the buildings behind are painted using paint with a semi-dry consistency.

Materials Used

- White tracing-down sheet (bought from an art shop) + 2H pencil
- 2 bristle brushes: 1 wide flat in (10mm), 1 small flat in (6mm), or less
- 1 soft-hair brush: small, round size 3, with tip cut off
- Designers' gouache: alizarin crimson, ultramarine blue, yellow ocher and permanent white
- Blue mount board
- Bathroom tissue

METHOD

Although the photograph (facing page, top right) appears dark and colorless, if you look closely at it you will find tonal changes. Any hint of color can be exaggerated – and even made up – as long as it looks good in the painting (it's called artistic license).

First, the photographic image is transferred to the board (see Transferring the Image, pages 20-21). Then an oil-painting technique is used, the reverse of the way we have been working so far, as the paint will be used a lot dryer in consistency. Painting on a colored surface means that white paint is relied on to achieve the lighter colors. The wide bristle brush and the three strong colors (not white at this stage) are used first, straight out of the tube. Because the paint will dry rapidly, it will need to be revived frequently with a little water.

The colors are adjusted, adding crimson in the warm areas and blue in the cooler areas, and yellow ocher is used to lighten the tones as far as possible, rather than using white. Next a touch of white is added as the shapes continue to be painted in, making the tones progressively lighter **(1)**.

2. Fairly dry paint is used for the rest of the building, with lighter and warmer tones to suggest reflected light off the shimmer.

The water area is painted in, up to and over the gondola. The paint is thinned with a little water where necessary, the top of the sky is painted in, and the color adjusted with white; a touch of ocher and red paint are used for the lighter area of sky and the board color is allowed to show through in places, to help unite the colors in the painting **(2)**.

With the smaller bristle brush and a touch more white, the lighter wave shapes are painted in, then the ocher roof, with yellow and white, and the highlights in the water – large, bold brush marks in the foreground, and the yellow highlights on the ocher roof facing the light, using the paint dry to give lots of texture. The colors are not used too bright – the lights will be built up gradually **(3)**.

The palette is cleaned and, with a strong dark mix of blue and crimson the right-hand shadow side of the gondola is repainted, warming the color as the light from the shimmer catches on

3. The water is painted in with horizontal strokes, then the sky, with very small amounts of white, red, and yellow added to lighten the mixture where the sky meets the horizon.

4. Brighter blue horizontal strokes are used to suggest wave shapes, and yellow mixed with white to paint in the shimmer and highlights on the buildings facing the sun.

5. Warm colors are used to suggest reflected light on the gondola, the distant boat, and the buildings, and the distant shimmer is brightened. Green wave shapes are suggested in the foreground, a few textured cloud streaks placed in the sky, and masts are painted in with a suggestion of highlights around them.

the back end. The small boat is painted in with warm, orange/red color, as it is surrounded by sparkling light, and the same color is used for the buildings affected by the bright light which is reflecting light into them. The shimmer is painted over with white and just a touch of yellow to brighten the color nearer the horizon (and the sun) and the texture of the paint used to suggest the sparkle **(4)**.

The long streaks in the sky are painted in as textures with ocher and orange mixes, then, using the small sable brush and a warm purple mix, highlights are added in by the lighthouse on the left and the boat masts. The brush marks are left showing intentionally – they describe the values becoming lighter and make the skies and buildings look more interesting – and part of the pleasure of looking at paintings is to enjoy the washes and brush marks **(5)**.

MORGAN SPORTS CAR

In the photograph (right) the light from above highlights the top of the car bonnet, the shiny chrome lamps, grill, and wheels. These will be the strongest whites in the painting and the strongest dark will be under the front wheel arch.

METHOD

For this demonstration an illustration technique is used, which is great for painting subject matter where accuracy and detail are important. First, the photographic image is traced off using a ruler where necessary, (see Transferring the Image, pages 20-21). Then, with a soft pencil, all the dark areas and some detail are drawn in, including the dark spaces between the spokes, to highlight them. There is no white on the palette to start with. The large, soft-hair brush is then used to paint a pale wash of yellow ocher over the drawing, covering the edges, to fix the pencil and get rid of all the white areas **(1)**.

Materials Used

- Tracing-down sheet (see pages 18-19) + 2H pencil
- Soft pencil (2B-4B)
- 2 soft-hair brushes: 1 large flat in (12mm), 1 small round, size 3, with tip cut off
- Designers' gouache: alizarin crimson, ultramarine blue, yellow ocher and permanent white
- Smooth watercolor board
- Ruler
- Bathroom tissue

1. The dark areas in the image are drawn in with a soft pencil, using varying strength of line and shading to pick out as much detail as possible from the photograph.

2. Working dark to light, a dark wash is used to paint in the front wheel arch and the tones are made progressively lighter and more colorful as the painting progresses.

Using the small soft-hair brush, and a dark wash, the strongest dark under the front wheel arch is painted. Any areas with reflected light are brightened, watering down the washes for the paler darks and adjusting the color with red and ocher as appropriate.

Next, the dark blue sections are painted in behind the lamps and rear wheel arch (blue with a touch of crimson) and the washes watered away as required to sculpt the shapes **(2)**.

The main shapes of the blue body work are painted in next, darker sections first, followed by paler sections. The blue is warmed with crimson to paint the hood and the wheels, including the area between the spokes. The green grass is suggested with a wash and, when dry, the shadow under the car is painted in **(3)**.

Now that the main shapes have been blocked in, the strong darks under the front wheel arch are painted over again, with a more solid paint mixture. The darks are then watered down to make them paler, and the sill and and doors painted in using a ruler (*see* Brushruling, page 17). Highlights on the blue bodywork are exaggerated to give the car more clarity, the washes on the bonnet softened to suggest the roundness of the bonnet, and purple tones used on the hood to bring out the shapes in it.

Using pure white, of a creamy consistency (not too wet) and a ruler where necessary, the whites of the window frame and the highlights in the mirrors, lamps, and number plate are painted in and some of the highlights in the spokes picked out. Finally, white paint is used around the shape of the front and rear of the car. A blue "cloud" shape is painted in the sky with a wash of blue and a touch of crimson (no white), then, using white with a touch of blue, the sky is painted up to the hood of the car to create some drama **(4)**.

This way of working (from the dark to light) is opposite to the watercolor style (from light to dark) and, by selecting the front wheel arch — a really dark area in the part of the car closest to us — then making all the other dark areas slightly paler, the car is given a three-dimensional feel.

3. Blue washes describe the paintwork, purple washes the hood, grill, and wheels.

4. The dark wheel arch is repainted and varying dark washes give the car more focus. Lastly, white paint is used to paint the highlights on all the chrome areas facing the sky.

SWAN

In the photograph (right) light comes from the left-hand side, half the neck is in shadow, and the neck itself casts a shadow across the swan's back. The strongest white areas will be the front of the head, the base of the neck and the front chest area of the body. The strongest darks are in the face.

METHOD

First, the photographic image is transferred to the green board using the white tracing-down sheet (*see* Transferring the Image, pages 20-21). Green mount board was chosen as there is a green undertone to the scene in the photograph. Next, using the large soft-hair brush, ultramarine blue is mixed with a touch of alizarin crimson and white and, using the paint quite wet, the darker sky color – reflected in the water in the foreground – is washed in. More white is added for the paler reflection in the distance and the brushstrokes are painted in the same direction as the movement in the water. The paint is washed over the swan, but the color is thin enough to allow the tracing and the green mount board color to show through **(1)**.

Materials Used

- White tracing-down sheet (bought from an art shop) + 2H pencil
- 2 bristle brushes: 1 wide flat in (10mm), 1 small flat in (6mm), or less
- 2 soft-hair brushes: small, round size 3, with tip cut off, 1 large flat ½in (12mm)
- Designers' gouache: alizarin crimson, ultramarine blue, yellow ocher and permanent white
- Green mount board
- Bathroom tissue

1. With a wide, soft-haired brush and using white mixed with blue and a touch of alizarin, washes are broadly painted in to suggest water.

2. A small, soft-haired brush is used to suggest the tree and swan reflections, lighter washes paint in the ripple in the water.

A little ocher is added to the mix and the
lighter patches are painted in on the water
and in the reflection of the swan's body.
Noting that the light areas reflect darker
and the dark areas reflect lighter, the color
is grayed by adding blue for the rest of the
body (experiment with the color mixing
– if a mixture looks badly wrong, it can be
painted over). The darker tree reflections in
the top part of the reference are suggested
– but not too darkly – with the brushwork
following the direction of the water movement
and indicating some ripple lines in the
foreground **(2)**.

Part of the palette is cleaned and fresh
water is used to mix a strong, dark, dryer
paint mixture. Using the small bristle brush,
the beak and face, and then the shadow-side
of the head and neck, are painted in with a
green/blue mix. The darker (shadow) areas
are painted first, then the lighter (sunlit)
areas on top **(3)**.

Next, thick dry paint is applied to the shadow
side of the body, to suggest texture and the
shapes of the wings, tail, feathers, and body.
More darks are suggested in the reflection in
the water. The more mixing that is done on the
palette, the more interesting it becomes and all
the colors can be revived and adjusted by adding
new color to them **(4)**.

3. Working dark to light, the dark shapes in the swan's head are painted and the neck shadows are
suggested, using thicker paint and a small bristle brush.

4. The feather shapes in the body are painted next, using a small bristle brush to describe the shapes that
make up the body.

5. Using white with a little ocher and very dry paint, the brushwork highlights the lighter side of the swan's body and tail.

6. The strong highlights in the head, neck, and body are painted in, then the white is darkened with color to paint the detail in the neck and the darker shapes in the reflection.

The light areas on the swan's back are painted in using dry white paint with a touch of yellow (noting that the angle of the body facing forward, towards the sun, catches the light more than the top of the body which faces the sky). A touch of blue is added while painting towards the top of the body and more yellow is painted on the tip of the tail. The light and shade are exaggerated in all areas, to add interest **(5)**.

The highlights on the top of the head and neck are painted in using white with a touch of ocher and, adding more ocher further down the head, the shadow side and back of the neck, where there is reflected light. The neck and shadow shape cast across the back are indicated in a gray/blue, then, reflecting the sky color, other reflected-light effects – such as the blue on the back of the head and the base of the neck joining the body – are painted in, together with a hint of feathers in the body. Lastly, with the small soft-hair brush, pure white is spotted in the highlight on the head and around the eye, and a touch of yellow is added for the top of the beak. No attempt has been made to match the color in the photograph – the shapes that make up the body and the color in the reference have been noted but the values exaggerated **(6)**.

LOCOMOTIVE

In the photograph (right) the sky color has been bleached out, and there is no strong sunlight. The light there is comes from above, so the strongest darks will be under the locomotive and the strongest lights on any shiny metallic parts near the front.

METHOD

First, the image is traced off (*see* Transferring the Image, pages 20-21) then, using the 4B pencil, the darkest areas in the scene are indicated. A yellow ocher wash is then painted over the whole board, so no white is showing **(1)**.

The lighter parts of each section of the locomotive and tracks are then washed in, bearing in mind that the trucks on the left are much lighter in color. Using a dark mix of blue, alizarin, and a touch of ocher, strong darks are added, the color changed to make it paler, warmer, or cooler as appropriate, so the rear of the locomotive appears to recede. An ocher wash is then painted over the building, a pale blue wash over the sky, and the cooling towers are suggested while the sky is wet **(2)**.

Materials Used
- Tracing-down sheet + 2H pencil
- Soft (4B) pencil
- 2 bristle brushes: 1 wide flat in (10mm), 1 small flat in (6mm), or less
- 2 soft-hair brushes: 1 large flat in (12mm), 1 small round, size 3, with tip cut off
- Designers' gouache in alizarin crimson, ultramarine blue, yellow ocher and white
- Smooth watercolor board
- Ruler
- Bathroom tissue

1. With a soft pencil, all the main dark areas are drawn in, looking hard into the shadows to bring out the detail.

2. Light washes are used to block in the main shapes of the locomotive, trucks, buildings, and towers.

3. Strong darks are painted under the front of the boiler and made paler and warmer to paint in the rest of the locomotive.

4. The trucks are suggested with paler darks to allow the locomotive to stand out and the rails are painted with warmer browns.

The undercarriage on the truck on the left is worked on, keeping the darks pale compared to the locomotive, then the detail in the tracks suggested, simplifying as much as possible and not making the dark areas too dark **(3 and 4)**.

Next the truck and the buildings behind and on the right are painted, keeping everything understated, to bring focus to the locomotive. The darks on the locomotive are worked on, and a little more detail painted in, re-stating the reds and putting in the greens on the coal tender. Some of the highlights are now suggested, by adding white to the palette on the locomotive and the lettering on the truck, using a brush-rule technique (*see* page 17), and the paint thin or more opaque as appropriate.

5. The darks are reaffirmed at the front of the locomotive and the tones refined to help it to stand out, while paler washes are used on the rear to make it recede into the background.

The sky is painted with a thicker mix of blue, white, and a touch of crimson, and the color blended into the previous washes. While the sky is wet, the cooling towers and the white smoke are painted in **(5)**.

With a hog-hair brush, the gravel between the tracks is added, using the texture of the paint to suggest the gravel. The building on the left is worked on with a soft-haired brush, ensuring that it is not made too dominant, and also the trucks on the left. Finally, the locomotive and the front tracks are worked on, painting the red front section in and darkening the strong darks on the locomotive and front tracks **(6)**.

6. Using white and a large soft-hair brush the sky is blocked in, and more textured paint with a bristle brush is used for the gravel between the tracks. White paint and a small, soft brush are used to indicate the highlights in the chrome and other reflected surfaces facing the sky.

PYRAMIDS, CAIRO

In the photograph (right) the light is coming from the right-hand side and I chose the darkest area for the painting to be the shadow under the hat, while the strongest light is in the white pattern on the cloth over the man's shoulder.

METHOD

An oil-painting technique is used here, so we start with the darkest color (no white) and work towards the lightest areas (with white) in a logical tonal progression. Treating every other tone lighter than the dark and darker than the light gives the painting depth, and painting on a gray, neutral-colored board will help the whites to really stand out.

First, the image is traced off (*see* Transferring the Image, pages 20–21). With the small bristle brush and quite thick paint, a dark color is mixed from the blue, crimson, and ocher. The dark areas are painted in, starting with the darkest area – the shadow under the man's hat. Textured brushwork is used, and the color adjusted to cooler and darker on the shadow side and warmer on the sunny side **(1)**.

Materials Used

- Tracing-down sheet + 2H pencil
- 2 bristle brushes: 1 wide flat in (10mm), 1 small flat in (6mm or less)
- 1 soft-hair brush: small round, size 3, with tip cut off
- Designers' gouache: alizarin crimson, ultramarine blue, yellow ocher and permanent white
- Smooth, light-gray board
- Ruler
- Bathroom tissue

1. The dark shapes are painted in, starting with the strongest darks under the man's hat, then becoming progressively lighter.

2. Washes are painted over all areas to suggest the local color and the shadow areas.

Some of the features in the camel's face and body are painted in, using ocher and brown washes (the colors are lightened like a watercolor at this stage, to get as much out of the three colors as possible, before introducing white). The blankets and rugs are filled in, the colors changed to prevent them looking identical **(2)**.

Next, the shapes in the camel's face and body and the shadows on the figure are filled in, using ochers and blues (no white). Washes are used to paint in the main shapes in the background **(3)**.

White is added to the palette and the sky painted in: starting at the top, blue with a touch of crimson is used, then more white, and a touch of ocher and crimson are added towards the horizon. The sand and pyramids are painted in with texture and subtle, pale tones of pink and purple, exaggerating the colors in the reference. The light areas in the man's clothing are painted out with blue grays **(4)**.

The highlights in the cloth on the man's shoulder (the strongest white) are painted in using white with a touch of ocher, then the tone is darkened slightly with blue and red for the shoes and sock. The other items of clothing are painted, and the color is adjusted to make the highlights darker **(5)**.

The highlights in the camel's face and body are painted next, but made darker than in the photograph. Some of the detail in the rugs is indicated using the small soft brush for fine strokes, and the bristle brush for textured marks **(6)**.

3. Adding tiny amounts of white, the cool shadows on the camel and man are indicated.

The strong darks are painted in, starting with the shadow under the man's hat, then the paler darks (warmed with crimson or cooled with blue), and adjustments made to the tones in the shadow areas as appropriate. The whip is painted in using a ruler, the highlights in the face are painted in with subtle browns, and any detail in the rugs and clothing that may be necessary. Finally, the strongest highlight on the man's shoulder is painted in, if necessary **(7)**.

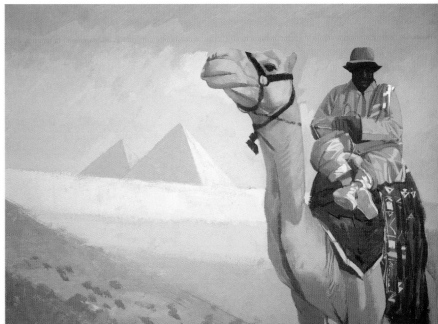

sky, pyramid, and sand are painted in using slightly wet paint for the sky, much dryer
xtured paint for the rest of the background. The man's clothes are indicated.

5. White mixed with a touch of ocher is used to paint the lightest area – the highlight on the cloth
on the man's shoulder – then the other light areas are progressively darkened with color.

hlights are painted in the camel's face and body with a lot more color than is suggested in the
graph, and detail is added to the rugs and blankets.

7. The strongest darks are painted over again, browns finish off the harness on the camel's
head, and detail is added as necessary.

TIGER ENTERING A POOL

In the photograph (right) the sunlight is low and coming from the right-hand side, casting a long shadow. This catches the white fur on the right side of the tiger's head to give the brightest highlight, while the dark stripes on the shadow side of the head are the strongest darks.

METHOD

Because the greatest points of contrast are close together, and the use of thick gouache and bristle brushes on the gray tinted board gives the fur lots of texture, the light color on the head really sings, making the tiger's head stand out.

First, the photographic image is transferred to the board (see Transferring the Image, pages 20–21). The dark areas on the tiger (stripes mainly) are drawn in using a soft pencil, also detail that was unclear at the trace-down stage, and the dark shadows behind the tiger **(1)**.

An oil-painting technique is used here, so the strong dark areas in the head are painted first and the color is made progressively lighter as the painting progresses.

Materials Used

- 2 bristle brushes: 1 wide flat in (10mm), 1 small flat in (6mm), or less
- 1 soft-hair brush: small, round size 3, with tip cut off
- Designers' gouache: alizarin crimson, ultramarine blue, yellow ocher and permanent white
- White tracing-down sheet (available from art shops)
- Hard pencil (2H)
- Soft pencil (2B–4B)
- Smooth gray board
- Bathroom tissue

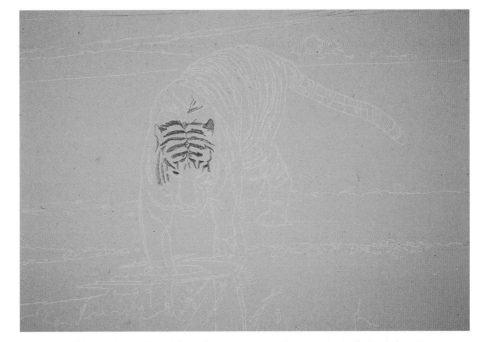

1. A soft pencil is used to draw in and shade the darker areas in the scene, to clarify the dark and the light stripes.

2. The darks are painted in, starting with the head and becoming paler and more colorful as they recede into the background.

Using just the three colors (no white yet) a strong dark is mixed from ultramarine, alizarin, and a touch of ocher. The stripes in deepest shadow on the left side of the head are painted first, using the paint reasonably opaque and the small bristle brush. For the stripes on the sunny side of the body, warmer brown tones – created by mixing small amounts of blue with orange – are used, noting that the stripes in sunlight are brighter and warmer, while those in shade are cooler and darker. The stripes are lightened by adding ocher to the darks – or even a little water – but not white **(2)**.

Once all the stripes have been indicated, a thinner paint is used to fill the areas in between with orange and light browns. With the larger bristle brush and the paint thin, cooler washes are added to the shadow areas, the background is blocked in making the bank facing us grayer and the shadow facing the sky (which reflects the sky color) bluer. All other areas are washed out with rough tones **(3)**.

Heavier mixes are now used to paint in the bank details and blue shadows, so that they contrast more against the tiger. Next, some grasses are broadly indicated in the foreground – allowing some of the gray board to show through – and the grass area on top and the pool are washed out. The textures in the tiger are adjusted to get as much mileage as possible from the three-color mixes. Now we start with the light areas and work back towards the darks. Part of the palette is cleaned and white introduced.

3. Without using white, orange-browns are mixed and used to fill in between the stripes. A cool wash is painted in the background.

4. All other areas are filled in with approximate color values and varying consistency of paint. Using white, the strongest lights are painted in.

5. The light areas are painted in, the whites become progressively less bright.

6. To make the tiger stand out more, the background darks are strengthened with textured strokes. Reflections are added.

7. Starting with the darkest area, the stripes are repainted – the tones adjusted as necessary – and the foreground textures are added.

A touch of ocher is added to it and, using a corner of the small bristle brush, the strong highlights are painted in on the right side of the face, then more ocher is added to indicate the highlights in the legs **(4)**.

This continues all over the tiger's body: the ocher is adjusted with red, touches of blue, and small amounts of white to describe the curves of the body, and the movement in the water and reflections are indicated. A purple is mixed, some white and a touch of ocher are added where necessary, and the cooler shadows painted in with this mix and textured brush strokes **(5)**.

The background is built up using bolder color (but no white) to make the tiger stand out and shapes with lots of texture are suggested within the shadows. The colors on the palette are adjusted for the water and the edge of the concrete wall is lost, to make it look like a bank made of earth with grasses overhanging. Some reflected lights in shadow areas are painted in on the tiger **(6)**.

A clean palette, fresh paint, and water are used to mix a strong dark and the darkest darks are repainted, the color adjusted with browns and dry paint, using the small soft brush. Some vegetation is painted in using the small bristle, keeping the foreground free and loose. Lastly, a small brush is used to indicate the whiskers – lighter on the right, with shadow color on the left **(7)**.

MALLARDS

Here, the light is coming from the top left, so the white highlights are on the part of the drake's body mostly facing this direction, and on the front part of his white collar. The darkest area in the painting could be the tail feather on the drake.

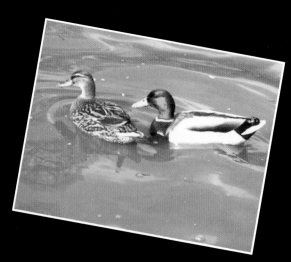

Materials Used

- White tracing-down sheet (available from art shops)
- Hard pencil (2H)
- 2 bristle brushes: 1 wide flat in (10mm), 1 small flat in (6mm), or less
- 2 soft-hair brushes: 1 wide flat ½in (12mm), 1 small, round size 3, with tip cut off
- Designers' gouache: alizarin crimson, ultramarine blue, yellow ocher, and permanent white
- Green mountboard
- Bathroom tissue

METHOD

Here, gouache is used to its full potential: big swirly washes for the water are made with a large soft brush, and thick-textured strokes with a bristle brush used for the ducks' feathers. Note how the light areas on the right-hand side of the male bird's body have bleached to white, making it look flat. A green mountboard was used for the painting, as a green hue underlies the colors in the water in the photograph, and it shows up the great versatility of the gouache colors, both washes and opaque color. First, the photographic image is transferred to the board using the white tracing-down sheet (see Transferring the Image, pages 20–21), and the chalky white line shows up really well on the dark board **(1)**.

1. White tracing-down paper is used to transfer the image onto the green mountboard.

2. White, mixed with blue and a touch of alizarin, is applied with a large soft brush and, with the paint a little wet, the big swirls in the water are painted.

With a soft-haired watercolor brush, ultramarine blue is mixed with a little white, and alizarin crimson added to subdue the brightness of the blue. The color is mixed to a milky consistency and the darker swirling pattern of the water painted in, adding more blue, ocher, or white, as appropriate. The brighter color is applied on top, but care is taken to avoid making the light areas too bright. The washes are painted over the outline of the birds, so no gaps show **(2)**.

The palette is cleaned, so no trace of the white is left and, with fresh paint, the three colors are used to paint in the ducks. The darkest areas - the blue/purples - first, then the red/browns and finally the ocher/browns. The color is lightened as much as possible without adding white, and the paint is used quite dry, out of the tube, with the small, flat bristle brush **(3)**.

3. With a mix of the three colors – no white to begin with – the patterns in the ducks' bodies are painted in.

4. Using white, the lighter patterns are painted on the left duck, but the shapes are not made too bright.

5. The same process is repeated on the drake, finishing off with strong highlights on his front. The reflections are added.

White is now added to the palette and the female bird worked on, first the darker areas, then the brighter (but not white) areas **(4)**.

So far, dark colors have been worked towards the light colors, but now the lightest areas are worked back towards the darks. Starting with the lightest area on the male – the shoulder – white is mixed with ocher and used very dry to paint the shoulder highlight, then the paint is rubbed into the purple shadow color. The two colors are blended to suggest the roundness of the bird's body, the beak, and the other light areas; purple is added to the paint where appropriate, for example in the male reflection, or ocher red as in his back. The female's reflected shape is now added.

With a clean palette the darks are again restated where necessary. The light areas on the female in the photograph have been ignored, allowing the highlight on the male to be the strongest highlight **(5)**.

EDWIN'S
PORTRAIT

The photograph (above) was taken in sunlight, which is casting light from above and slightly to the left, giving good descriptive shadows. The lightest area is the highlight in the right eye and the strongest dark is under the rim of the cap.

METHOD

First, the photographic image is transferred to the board (see Transferring the Image, pages 20–21). The soft pencil is then used to draw in the dark shapes of the features, following the direction of the eyebrow hairs and beard, and softening the line where appropriate. The pencil drawing is brush-washed over using the wide soft-hair brush and the wash taken over the edges of the drawing, to fix the pencil and get rid of the whites **(1)**.

If you half close your eyes and look at the reference, you will see the big shapes – eye sockets, cap shadow, cheeks, and neck. These are painted in using ocher with a touch of red (no white on the palette yet) and adding blue where appropriate. The cap, clothing, beard, and hair are then blocked in **(2)**.

Materials Used

- Tracedown sheet (see Making a Tracedown Sheet, pages 18–19)
- 2H pencil for tracing down
- 2 soft-hair brushes: 1 wide, flat ½in (12mm), 1 small round, size 3, with tip cut off
- Designers' gouache: alizarin crimson, ultramarine blue, yellow ocher, and permanent white
- Soft (4B) pencil
- Watercolor board
- Bathroom tissue

1. The features are drawn in with a soft pencil, describing them with the direction of the pencil marks.

2. Light washes suggest the underlying color in the face and features (the washes are built up in thin layers, as they are easier to darken than to lighten).

3. The shadow areas are built up and more soft washes used to build up the features in the face.

4. The mid-tones are worked on, watering out and softening them to describe the contours of the face, and the washes are built up gently. They shouldn't be rushed.

A dark color is mixed from crimson and a touch of ocher, and the dark shadows in the eyes, nose, beard, and chin are painted in, using the small soft brush. The color is adjusted as appropriate: red is added to the shadow on the top of the lip and the mixture is warmed up with crimson and ocher to paint in the cap shadow, and cooled off with blue for the hair **(3)**.

The whole face is worked over, without finishing any area off, and the features gradually built up with thin washes. Observing the way the light describes the roundness of the cheeks

and nose, red is added to the ocher for the warm flesh tones and blue to the mix for the pale browns. Blue-grays are used to paint in the shape of the moustache and beard, then the cap and clothing are painted in **(4)**.

The details of the eyes are now built up with more darks and browns, and the shadow under the cap is strengthened and some of the detail painted in **(5)**.

The palette is cleaned, white is added to it and, with clean water and the small brush, a tiny touch of yellow is added to the white, which should make a light, creamy consistency.

With this mix the highlight in the right eye is painted in. A touch more yellow paint is added for the light by the left eye (joining the nose), some highlight on the left cheek is painted in, and the mixture darkened again with more yellow to paint in the highlight on the nose. A touch of blue is added to the white and some of the hairs in the beard are suggested – brighter on the left side, more shadowy on the right (to avoid the highlights on the face looking too flat). Finally, using clean water and pure white paint, the area around the head is painted out, to give the portrait a crisp edge **(6)**.

5. Some detail in the hat and jumper is added, but the photograph is not copied exactly. The shadows describe the hat and face, so those are painted with clarity.

6. White is used with touches of color to add crisp highlights to the face, and pure white is used to sharpen up the face against the white background.

Stan's secluded studio in his garden,
where he runs classes, paints, and has
even held exhibitions.

ACKNOWLEDGMENTS

DEDICATION

To the chance meeting with Martin Sharrocks who gave me the final push
to put the book together, to Geoff Sewell and all my students past and present
who have faith that what I do has some value, and to my wife Christine and son
Alan to let them know this is what I am best at.

The Golden Retriever demonstration on pages 86-89 is dedicated to the
memory of Ben.

PHOTOGRAPHIC CREDITS

All photographs taken by the author, apart from those on the following pages:
Anthony Bailey (© **GMC Publications**), pp. 15, 16, 18, 22, 24 and 32;
Andrea Bridgeman: p. 60; **Pam Elmer:** p. 40; **Jill Harrington:** p. 72;
Joy Poole: p. 56; **Paul Rivers – Latham**: p. 48; **Mike Scholey:** p. 102;
Roy and Jackie Shearey: p. 82; **David Tanner:** p. 94.

GMC Publications would also like to thank Tashtori Arts & Crafts, Lewes, for the
loan of pencils used in the photographs on pages 15 and 17.

INDEX

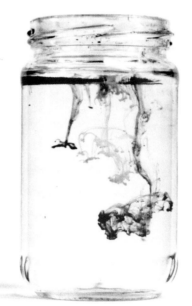

To place an order, or to request a catalog, please contact:

GMC Publications
Castle Place, 166 High Street, Lewes, East Sussex
BN7 1XU, United Kingdom

Tel: 01273 488005 Fax: 402866
Website: www.gmcbooks.com

Orders by credit card are accepted